How To Raise A Leader

7 Essential Parenting Skills For Raising Children Who Lead

Frank Dixon

from various sources. Please consult a licensed professional before attempting any techniques outlined in this book.

By reading this document, the reader agrees that under no circumstances is the author responsible for any losses, direct or indirect, that are incurred as a result of the use of the information contained within this document, including, but not limited to, errors, omissions, or inaccuracies.

Table of Contents

Introduction

Trailblazer–such a fascinating and inspirational word. They ignite the flames, discover novel paths, pave new roads, and light up a tunnel with their confidence, integrity, honesty, and positive approach. They know if they set their mind, anything is possible. They are the heroes of their own story. They try and they succeed. They aim and they hit their target. They make a wish and it gets fulfilled.

If anything, they are leaders in all walks of life.

Since there is no proof of a leadership gene, it can be assumed that we all can be leaders with some training and experience. This also means that we can train and raise our kids to be one as they grow up. Effective leadership skills don't just help people excel in their field of work, it helps them take control of all areas in their life.

Besides, all the qualities that a leader possesses are the ones any parent would want to instill in their child. Leaders are authentic, critical thinkers, have charismatic personalities, and an urge to serve others. These are qualities every parent wants to foster in their child. As they are young and curious, so is their brain. It is like a sponge ready to soak up all the information it can about new things. Research suggests that the more targeted and varied external stimuli, the healthier the brain grows. When we are born, we have approximately 100 billion brain cells. As we grow older, these cells form connections with one another and create memories. The more connections, the improved memory problem-solving skills, and cognitive function. Therefore, as parents, we should try to introduce our children to the right skills and environment so that they pick up the right passions, which will stimulate their growing minds.

If we talk about kids in general, we know that they are entrepreneurs from the very get-go. They have the three things common in all entrepreneurs–curiosity, enthusiasm, and ambition. Unluckily, they lose these over time. They exchange a nice and steady job for their big dreams and goals.

But with changing times, we are seeing a new trend develop. Steady jobs are losing their essence. More and more people are drawn towards an entrepreneurial journey. They want to be a part of something bigger, original, and high-paying. To seek that, they work on their ideas, read the market, assess a need, and set up a business right from their homes. They look for investment opportunities, work side-gigs, and still make time for others in their lives. By 2020, up to 43% of the U.S. workforce is part of the gig economy, suggests one research (Gillespie, 2017).

Being an entrepreneur requires being a leader too. The leader isn't just a businessman or a sleeping partner but someone ready to change the world and deliver what society needs. The leader is motivated and wants to inspire others to do the same. The leader is honest, compassionate, and curious. They are ambitious and enthusiastic, the very skills your little one has right now.

So how about you put them to good use and encourage your child to keep the curiosity, commitment, and passion alive?

In this book, we will discover this and a lot more to help parents raise kids that are ready to take charge of their lives and lead others to change the status quo too. Together, we shall explore many strategies, activities, and practical tips to help parents both new and experienced to raise emotionally-intelligent, self-reliant, and confident kids.

So let's dive right in and learn to tailor-made a leader fit to be a trailblazer.

Chapter 1:

The Making of a Leader

For a leader, a challenge may arise at any time. Whether you react to the threat or respond to it determines if you are a true leader. Leaders respond strategically. They use their expertise, wisdom, and intelligence to guide them.

A child is no different. Their reactions and responses govern the outcome. Sometimes, they succeed, and sometimes, they fail. To be effective leaders, they must know how to tackle challenges and unforeseen situations strategically. Here, the word strategically denotes our cognitive ability. How we think influences our decision-making ability. For example, if a child has to decide between wearing formal shoes or casual ones to an event, they must know how to weigh the pros and cons of each and not go with appearance alone. This ability to think clearly and with biases aside is something that can be taught.

This first chapter closely explores the making of a leader and what other qualities differentiate them from the lot. We also look at how parents can develop those qualities in their kids and raise them to be one.

But first, let's look at who a leader is.

Who is a Leader?

The essence of any effective leadership lies in being able and inspirational. Effective leadership stems from ideas, both borrowed and original, that are later communicated in ways that engage. An effective leader has followers who listen and live by what their leader has to say. A leader can be a source of inspiration in many forms such as religion, career, or even relationships. Their goal is to trigger action and lead others to their desired goals. Such power must be exercised with care and caution.

People look up to a leader to learn how to live their life. They act as their leader does and abide by the rules set by them. This means that the leader must have a strong convincing and charismatic power that urges people to give up their innate beliefs and follow the ones of their leader.

Leaders are critical thinkers. They embark on journeys of the coming time. They see ahead of their competition, the market, and the economy and set new trends in place. They know how to use the resources at their disposal in the best way possible to help themselves and others excel and benefit from them.

Leaders have to have a purpose and agenda too that offers welfare for all. They can't act tyrant or be self-consuming. They think about the greater good and ensure all their followers remain safe. Their ways of practicing their power aren't inhumane or destructive. They don't take pleasure in hurting others or taking advantage of them. Leaders don't buy followers. People devote themselves to follow one of their free wills. Leaders can positively impact others around them.

A leader also has sharp focusing skills as they can pinpoint processes that need improvement and get like-minded people to push their ideas forward. Leaders put others first and genuinely hope to make a change for the better. They aren't just intrinsically motivated, their empathy and connection with others motivate them to do better. Leadership isn't a gene that only a few people possess. It is a gift that some choose to give themselves. Leaders look for people with diverse backgrounds so that they can have different perspectives to look at. Leaders work to bring people together.

In the following chapters, we shall put all these skills to the test and learn from the life of the greatest leaders and the obstacles they overcame to become a name the world will never forget.

Leaders are Made Not Born

As we already established that leaders are made and not born, teaching young minds about leadership becomes pivotal and quite frankly, a necessity. The journey is hard but we have all the amazing life stories to inspire and guide us in our quest to raise a leader. It all starts with choosing a niche your child is passionate about and nurturing it. For example, your child may like to speak and engage with others. They may be good at making friends and getting people to follow them. This suggests that they have great public speaking and persuasion skills. They have the power to say what's on their mind without hesitation and prove their point using both logic and emotion. Any great persuasive argument has both. Once you have identified an area of expertise, your goal is to give them more opportunities to excel in it. For instance, you can encourage them to take part in school debates or take them to places that offer acting or speaking classes. You can watch and rehearse with them the greatest speeches ever delivered. You can also role-play where they act as your leader and you act as their follower. You can also talk to them about the many qualities a good leader has other than effective persuasion and communication skills so that they may practice them too.

This is an example of how you can work with them as a team and raise them to put-perform all the others. Other than that, you can also instill positive leadership qualities in them using the following strategies.

A Change of Focus

A leader is always concerned more about what's the right solution to resolve a problem than pointing out who's right. In the face of misunderstandings or challenges, a leader reexamines their vision, values, activities, responsibilities, and goals. Leaders aren't just concerned about the end goal but rather how they can make their team or followers reach there with harmony and cooperation.

Therefore, teach your child to look at the bigger picture and not let small setbacks or challenges undermine their confidence and set them off their path to success. They should be taught to not lose heart and blame others for their miscalculations and failures because that won't make them accomplish their vision.

Have a Shared Goal

Another important quality of a leader is that they possess the skills needed to persuade and influence others to have a common goal. This means that a leader doesn't only think about their gains but of what others can get out of it too. For them, their team always comes first. They promote the principles of teamwork and appreciate those who show flexibility.

Your child should be taught the same. Today's world is the world of cooperation. Your child must know how to share things, be compassionate, and show empathy. They should understand that their decisions affect others too.

See Yourself as the Competition

Great leaders compete with themselves. They aren't afraid to hire people better than themselves in their team. They only focus on themselves and their improvement. They are concerned about whether they have added value to their skills and processes. They don't compare themselves with others in their field. This is what allows them to set new standards and become more proficient in whatever they do.

A child should also have this level of confidence and self-assurance in their abilities. They should know that their only competition is themselves. They should be motivated to work harder tomorrow and the next day. They shouldn't feel envious when someone in their class gets higher marks than them and works on improving themselves alone.

Set a Good Example

Leaders learn through experience. They aren't born with the trait to rule and mentor others. A leader knows what others want when they want it and how to give it to them. They set a good example for others to follow.

As a parent, you should aim for the same with your child. You should set a good example for them to follow. This requires being an ideal and disciplined parent that stays true to their commitments, doesn't lie or keep secrets, and dedicates their life for the betterment of others. You can also read to them about famous world leaders and their lives to motivate them to do the same.

Never Quit Learning

Leaders never stop learning. They ensure to continue to enhance their skills throughout their careers or job field. They believe that learning is an endless process and every new day comes with more wisdom and knowledge.

Every child should feel the same. They should feel motivated to learn new things and expand their horizon. They should be encouraged to hone their existing skills to become the best version of who they are.

Put Ideas into Action

Leaders aren't just effective communicators. They don't brag about what they can or can't do. Instead, they do it and then wait for the world to decide if they have succeeded or not. They are doers and go-getters. They don't sit around and delegate. They lead their team by being front-liners. They bring their ideas to life and embark on new journeys every day. Their willingness to try and make the world a better place is what sets them apart.

You should teach your child the same. They shouldn't be all talk and no work. They should only keep promises that they can keep and take on things they feel confident in doing. They should know that ideas can die in the head if not approached with determination. You can help them by setting realistic expectations for them.

Chapter 2:

The 7 Essential Parenting Skills for Raising Children Who Lead

If you are interested in teaching your child how to be an effective leader, there is little teaching involved. The reason I say this is that kids already have all the qualities and skills required to lead. All they need is some nurturing and passion to keep doing what they do and be who they are. Besides, most of the learning they will do is through experience, which turns out to be the best teacher there is. Leaders are self-made. If we talk about business settings, we notice that most of them start with crappy jobs. They volunteer to take on more which suggests they are initiators. They take over when something goes wrong and cleanup which suggests they have strong mentoring skills. Their learning doesn't stop after a seminar or workshop which signifies that they value learning above all. They look for inspiration from others' life and internalize the lessons one learns after overcoming hardships. This makes them great thinkers and exceptional problem-solvers.

They don't always win nor have it laid out for them. They fail. Many times.

But they rise again, like a phoenix rising from the ashes. They view failures and setbacks as lessons and look at how they can use that failure to fuel them for the success they desire. The examples are many. If we apply all these quality traits to someone like Thomas Jefferson, Abraham Lincoln, Mother Teresa, Winston Churchill, or Martin Luther King, we see that all of them build a name for themselves. Not all of them were born rich or had their parents supporting their careers. They made themselves of value. They chose to work hard, deliver, and change the status quo. They displayed great courage in the face of hardships and never stopped trying.

So the question is simple. What qualities do you need your child to possess and hone to become a leader of tomorrow? Luckily, the answers are all there. And it is time; we take a sneak peek at them.

Visionaries and Trendsetters

Leaders tend to be visionaries. They aren't followers or managers; instead, they lead with a positive attitude. They do the undoable. They make the unthinkable possible. They are creative souls that love to be challenged and tested from time to time. They aren't like everyone. They think outside the box. Their curiosity and hunger for more knowledge push them forward in all their quests.

Optimistic and Resilient

A leader doesn't give up in the face of failures. Leaders are always positive about themselves and others. They choose to see the good in others. They know that, throughout the journey, they will be challenged and tried but that doesn't make them scared of giving up on their course. They simply look for premeditated solutions to their problems. Great leaders never lose their calm and are logically-driven, meaning, they don't let their poor judgment get the best of them. Whenever they face a setback, they take one step back and rethink their strategy from the beginning.

Problem-Solvers

Leaders are also problem-solvers. They are great thinkers. They spend their idle time reading and researching about the things they don't know. They are committed to honing their skills and become a master at everything they do. They have learning agility which tells them what to do when they don't know what to do. They come out a victor in unfamiliar circumstances. They learn this through years of practice, effort, and experience.

Adherence to Principles

Leaders don't stop or return after having covered half the journey. They have strong beliefs and values guiding them. They stick to their word and remain committed to what they have set their mind to. They have a razor-sharp focus and fully engage themselves in whatever they are doing. We can all learn a few things from them.

Honest and Effective Communicators

Leaders know that communication and honesty are intertwined. They use honesty to communicate with their followers in a variety of ways from coaching them to transmitting new information. They are effective listeners as well which is why they can decipher the needs of others so expertly. They can read people and persuade them using their effective communication skills.

Empathetic

Leaders are empathetic and humble in their ways. Empathy has become an integral part of our lives today. Even in the business world, recruiters are more captivated by one's soft skills, of which empathy is one. Today's world is the world of collaboration. People must have the patience to work with one another and avoid conflicts as much as possible. Luckily, great leaders know how to win people using empathy and compassion. They are always ready to listen and respond to the needs of others and experience what they are experiencing.

Humbleness

Leaders empower others and motivate them to change their lives for the better. They have an unparalleled will that stops at nothing when it comes to causes bigger than them. They are ambition but for others. They think for the greater good and that is one reason people follow them devotedly. Sometimes, they forget about themselves and sacrifice the best time of their lives to find justice for others.

Now that we have these seven skills jotted down, let's see how these can be cultivated and nurtured in kids so that they can be raised as leaders in their lives.

Chapter 3:

Leaders Are Visionaries

and Trendsetters

In a world where the information lies at the fingertips of our hands, YouTube tutorials to guide us through something step by step, cheat codes for video games to pass difficult levels, engaging online games that keep children glued to the screens for hours, toys that come accompanied with instructional booklets, and books that offer all the advice we could ever need, it is extremely hard to make children think out of the box and do things that are original and new.

But we can always encourage them to seek newness. Remain curious and pursue things with intrigue. Never give up trying or be discouraged by a setback. Look at the bigger picture and channel their inner goodness to do something positive for others. After all, this is how trendsetters change the world.

Take Elon Musk as an example–a leader with a fervent mind and eagerness to know the unknown. Elon Musk is a great leader, by all means. Elon Musk comes from a South-African background, raised in the American dream. In 2021, he surpassed Jeff Bezos, the owner of Amazon as the wealthiest man on Earth. He founded X.com in 1999, commonly known as PayPal today. In 2002, he launched SpaceX and sent a rocket to the International Space Station in 2012. He also founded Tesla Motors in 2003. He earned the title of a multimillionaire in his early 20s when he sold his startup company to Compaq Computers.

Or perhaps, look at the life of Bill Gates that is a tale full of compromises, failures, and a determined mind. Today, very few people can compete with the genius that he is. He saw a computer for the first time when he was 13. Like most of us, he paid to use it and whenever he ran out of money, he would hack the system to use it for free. He came from a middle-class family and at an early age, revealed flashes of brilliance in entrepreneurship and business. By the time he turned 15, he started his own business with his friend Paul Allen and in 1975, they both co-founded Microsoft. Undoubtedly, he poured his heart and soul into it and made it a ginormous company with his incredible vision and unrivaled work ethic. Ever since then, he hasn't stopped at anything and proves to be one of the best examples of people who think out of the box and achieve the unachievable.

Being creative is one of the best qualities to have. Children are born with it. Everything piques their interest. As a parent, you need to nurture this quality and encourage them to think outside the box. But enough with the term already, what does it mean and why is it so important to develop?

Thinking Outside the Box: The Need of Today

A lot of people assume that thinking outside the box is a mindset but it is more than that. It is a lifestyle where you allow creativity to flourish. When you think outside the box and excel, it is because you have found something you love to do. When you do something that you are passionate about, you constantly think about how you can do it better. For example, if a child loves to paint or draw, they will keep looking to improve. They will want to have the best paint brushes and high-quality paints to fill their canvas with colors.

Thinking outside the box also means that you are willing to step out of your comfort and do things that you wouldn't otherwise attempt doing. This requires courage and going against yourself too. You leap and risk everything dear to you without any guarantees that what you need will be yours or not.

Kids should be motivated to do the same. Of course, not literally but they should be pushed to try new things and feel confident when approaching them. It is the need of today. Thanks to the advent of the internet and social media portfolios, our basic thinking has been stripped entirely. We have been modeled into robots, follow others blindly, and do things by the book so that we can have reached a certain standard. We put our kids into rich schools, make them take up curricula they have little interest in, only to earn them some extra credit. We try to manage every aspect of their lives using helicopter parenting, aka ripping away their consent and right to agree and disagree to things. What we fail to realize is the long-term impact of it. They become so used to doing things to please others that they kill every little bit of creativity inside. They aim to win everyone's heart by being the perfect child and play by the rules set for them. This dependency comes with a price, of course.

They never learn to take initiative on their own and rely on others for validation. In short, they never learn to become effective leaders.

What we are essentially doing is trying to fit them in a custom-made box when we should be forcing them to step out of it. The world fears individualism and therefore, tries to pigeonhole us into conformist and conventional thought so that we may die without having a purpose in our lives.

But is this the kind of life we want for our children? Do we want them to end up living a lie? Therefore, start preaching to them to step outside the box and bring something new to the table. The world is searching for pioneers and inventors. It isn't looking for college graduates with a 3.9 GPA without any confidence or purpose. The only people who have made a mark in this world are the ones who thought differently. Innovation drives humanity forward. If it weren't for those who tried to change the status quo, we would still be without transport, the internet, or even electricity.

Thinking outside of the box gives a child an edge over the others. They become problem-solvers and innovators. They can approach things in different ways and give their creativity an expressive outlet. Thinking untraditionally means that you are ready to consider different and aboriginal methods and solutions. Thinking in this manner can have a powerful impact on our child's professional and interpersonal life.

Some of the benefits of thinking outside the box include:

- Changing how things are leads to innovations. Think about it, if everyone accepted things as they are, we would still be living in the Stone Age. If we keep things as they are and do not seek change or improvement, the world will come to an end. When we question things constantly and work on improving on the original design, we give ourselves a chance to grow and excel.

- We also achieve a greater perspective. The world is a small place for the shy and close-minded. Expanding your horizons means expanding how you view the world. A broader perspective means a chance to become receptive to different ideas and solutions. It makes the impossible possible.

- It makes room for more creativity and problem-solving. It allows you to seek new ways to do things and become limitless. It helps you stand out and approach things from newer angles. The ability to think untraditionally is surely an asset for anyone, young or adult.

Encouraging Curiosity and Thinking outside the Box in Kids

Thinking outside the box is a paradigm shift. Psychologists label it as creative illumination or complete liberation. Being able to think out of the box unleashes creativity and innovative thinking in children. It helps them generate new ideas, explanations, and thoughts to view the world differently.

To promote this, there are several things you can do.

- Ask open-ended questions. Sometimes, as parents, we become so involved in our children's lives that we begin to answer on their behalf. If someone asks them something, we are quick to respond. This prevents children from forming their thoughts and opinions. It makes them more reliable for you. Firstly, let them lead on their own. Wait for them to form an idea or thought that their mind comes up with.
- Secondly, make your questions open-ended and inventive. Don't ask them things that can only be answered in "yes or nos." Let them come up with explanations by asking them what they

think about something or how would they approach or resolve it. This will encourage introspection and build focus and concentration.

- Add in ample opportunities for creative play. There are many age-appropriate activities that you can engage your tiny tot in to make them let their creative side show. Children need time to fully engage in something and lose themselves. Keep them engaged in games and activities that challenge their brain like puzzles, board, or card games.

- Let them fail over and over again to build stamina and resilience. Making mistakes and admitting to them takes guts. But what requires more strength is thinking about new solutions to resolve a problem. Your children need to rely on themselves to seek answers. And what better teacher than failure to guide them?

- Reduce screen time and substitute it with other, more creative activities during playtime. If they insist on watching television, watch with them movies, shows, and cartoons that project good leadership skills by the lead characters. You can even have a chat with them about how they felt after watching it and whether they felt inspired by the main lead or not for depicting excellent leadership skills.

- Let them color out of the lines. This advice comes from Sandra Fisher, an assistant professor of early-childhood education at Kutztown University. Sandra believes that when children are asked to color in between the lines or dictate how they should solve a math problem, it limits their creativity. They aren't able to express themselves or explore possible solutions. It also prevents them from making mistakes, which we already know, is pivotal for their growth.

Chapter 4:

Leaders Are Optimistic and

Resilient

Did you know J.K Rowling's first Harry Potter draft was rejected twelve times before a publishing firm decided to give it a go?

Or do you know that in 1928, Walt Disney was threatened by his partner Charles Mintz that if he didn't accept his terms and worked at reduced pay, he would cut all ties with him? He chose to part ways respectfully and start his own company and bring a new character to light: Mickey Mouse.

A lot of times, our children are faced with the conundrum of viewing the glass as half empty or half full. They are soon to lose heart when things don't go their way which means they are more pessimistic than hopeful of their chances at success.

But if they kick things off with a positive attitude, which is another important quality of great leaders, then there is a chance that success will find them itself. Being positive means that we remain calm, steady, and hopeful. We are aware of what negative self-talk and negative thinking can do to our brain, body, and soul. It corrupts it with doubt, low self-esteem, and poor self-worth. Children feel like they aren't good enough or strong enough to overcome obstacles on their own and end giving up.

However, if they are taught to see the positive in everything, there is a chance that they might train their brain to eliminate negative thinking and believe that anything is possible. A positive approach takes away the blame we put on ourselves or others when things go wrong. A positive and optimistic approach keeps us in control of our emotions.

The Perks of Having a Positive Outlook of Life

All the greatest leaders are legends for the same reason. No matter how dark or unexpected things got, they stayed positive and hopeful of a better tomorrow. They decided they won't let minor setbacks or failures deter them from their path. They stayed true to themselves, their value systems, and possessed a positive attitude.

A positive outlook towards life is a state of mind, an attitude that allows children to expect good things and envision success. Focusing on the positive doesn't mean that we turn a blind eye to all the negativity. It simply means that we choose to see past it and still hope for success. The benefits of staying positive are multifold. On top of the list of these benefits is happiness. As parents, the happiness of our children is one of the most important things. We want to raise them to be happy with who they are, how far they have come, and what they have accomplished.

Other than that:

- Thinking positively leads to an active and curious mind. Positivity creates endless possibilities. Kids can become more receptive to finding new information. This was examined in one experimental research study on self-belief (Syahrial et al., 2020). Two groups of students participated. The researchers looked at which students encountered problems in their learning and which students actively pursued it. Based on the findings, those with a positive attitude were more drawn towards finding new information as opposed to those who had a fixed mindset and pessimistic approach.
- This means that a positive approach helps one take on challenging tasks better and counter their negative feelings better.
- Optimistic children also tend to have more friends. They enjoy better social lives because they are the kind of people others want to hang around with. Think about it, would you like to

be friends with someone that only focuses on the negatives of something? Surely, they make everyone around them depressed. We all want to surround ourselves with people who bring out the best in us, are cheerful, upbeat, and make us feel good about ourselves.

- Then, overcoming challenges also becomes easier when you approach them with a positive and motivated mindset. Great leaders and businessmen all have exceptional grit and resilience. They aren't afraid of minor setbacks because they know a better tomorrow waits. This is all because they can regulate their negative emotions without losing their positivity.

- Next, it promotes happiness. We all want our children to be happy with who they are. A positive attitude is linked with increased feelings of happiness and well-being. Happiness doesn't come from materialistic things; it has to come from within. When we think positively, our responses become positive too. This promotes peace of mind and harmony.

- It also boosts self-confidence in children. Children who feel they are good enough feel better about themselves. They treat themselves with love and respect and don't shy away from others. This ingrained confidence in their appearance, skills, and abilities promotes inner strength and they can come out of their self-limiting beliefs.

- A positive attitude also improves emotion regulation in kids. When kids repeatedly see everything as a blunder, catastrophe, or failure, their emotions spiral out of control. According to one study, children that can remain positive despite the negativity around them can regulate their emotions better (Levens & Gotlib, 2012).

- Finally, it promotes the building of resilience and grit. Resilience can be defined as our ability to face and move on from a traumatic event, threat, setback, or adversity. Building resilience teaches children to face their demons and fears with a strong head and move on. It facilitates them in the management of stress, uncertainty, and stress. There is an abundance of research that links positive thinking with resilience. When children are taught resilience they can bounce back from any negative event using positive thinking. As per research (Tugade et al., 2004), higher resilience also promotes better health both physical and mental. Resilient people can reduce the risk of many life-threatening diseases and experience fast healing and recovery.

- So how about we learn to build resilience and a positive outlook at the same time? Surely, they both go hand in hand.

Building Resilience – Learn to Move On!

Children can be prone to trivial setbacks and losses. They may soon give up or fail to counter their negative emotions after a loss. We have all seen them flip a board game when they neared a loss. They lose temper, have a fit of crying, and scream at the top of their lungs. This isn't the most ideal way to deal with a failure or loss. Emotional pain and anxiety can sometimes get the best of them but if you want to raise a leader, you will have to teach them to work it out and develop a positive attitude. Parents must teach children to fight back, move on, and build resilience. There are many ways to do that and it all starts with the labeling of negative emotions so that the child knows what emotion is what. Emotions can run hot when stress kicks in. Labeling emotions is the first step towards teaching appropriate responses. Once they can identify what emotion they are experiencing, they can know how to cope with it. Also, let them know that it is normal to have overwhelming feelings at times but if they want to be a champion in life, they will have to learn to manage them.

Apart from that, nurture a positive self-view in them. Celebrate small wins so that the child feels optimistic and happy. If they are stuck at something and all set to give up, remind them of the times when they stayed committed and won. Use their accomplishments as a means to build inner strength and confidence. This is how you can teach them to trust their gut and make sensible decisions that come right from their mind and are not driven by their emotional distress.

Next, you must demonstrate excellent coping skills yourself so that they may learn from you. Set a good example of how you handle everyday stress and anxiety and make it through the day without losing your calm. Sit down with them and discuss healthy coping mechanisms to relieve their frustration and anger.

At the same time, you must encourage healthy risk-taking so that they can experience new things. You don't have to parent them all the time. Let them explore and learn from their mistakes by allowing them to make them. Healthy risk-taking is an excellent way to develop independence and build grit in children.

Aim to promote the positive side of things and be appreciative when they do something extraordinary. Children, in general, crave attention and appreciation. They want to feel valued, included and loved. One of the best ways to do that is by highlighting their successes and effort. Even when they make a mistake or fail at something, refuse to see it as one and praise them for trying.

Finally, let them know that they can always count on you and others for help when they need it. Sometimes, kids give up because they lack proper guidance and instructions. They make a mistake, get confused, and refuse to try again. Therefore, always offer help when you find them stuck at something. But be aware, this doesn't mean that you problem-solve for them. Just show support and be of help if they ask for it.

Chapter 5:

Leaders Are Problem-Solvers

If you wish to make your mark in this world, know that all great leaders throughout history became the greatest because they weren't afraid to solve problems and face challenges. Take Martin Luther King for example. Luther is arguably one of the most prominent names of the 20th century and remembered for his equal rights mass movement that inspired a generation. He led an entire civil rights movement, inspired by Mahatma Gandhi's non-violent activism. Being raised under the strict US segregation laws, he identified a problem i.e. racial discrimination, and ended institutional segregation throughout the country. He was awarded the Nobel Peace Prize for his contribution to make lawmakers rethink racial equality.

Another example we can learn from is of the man who led his men into the Second World War and won it for them. It is none other than Winston Churchill, who happens to be an important leadership figure in modern history. His speeches and dedication didn't only inspire the nation to stay strong in the face of danger but also motivated the allied forces to stand their ground and give their best. He knew that the only thing the British nation lacked was some much-needed enthusiasm and encouragement. He is also credited with halting fascist movements in the country and protecting democracy in Europe.

The reason to put forth these examples of great men is to make you see how important quality problem-solving is for children today. A great leader identifies a problem, uses their wisdom and expertise to come up with ideal solutions, and implements them to improve the state of their business, kingdom, or countrymen.

Therefore, in this chapter, we shall focus on why you need to help kids' problem-solve and keep that curiosity alive.

Problem-Solving and Success

As we have previously looked at how problem-solving is of great essence in the upbringing of a child, here, I want to focus on a more specific aspect of it, i.e. success. What is the connection between developing good problem-solving skills and success, given that there is any?

Our kids face new challenges every day. These problems can range from academics to sports, to interpersonal connections. Some days they have a hard time doing math, other days they fight with someone in class. Some days they have all the answers to every day and other days, they struggle with the most basic ones. When they are young, they have little knowledge of how to brainstorm ideas. They follow in the footsteps of others and do as they do. However, when they come across a problem that stops them in their steps, they freak out. Since they lack the will and determination, they avoid taking action. Instead of putting their energy into resolving the problem, they waste their time avoiding it. This is one of the few reasons some kids excel in school and some don't. This is also the reason why some kids are quick to make friends and some find it difficult to blend in.

Another important thing to note is that when kids lack the basic problem-solving skills, they spring into actions that are based on impulse. Meaning, they put little effort into thinking about the pros and cons and do what feels right to them. Although there is nothing wrong with believing in you, children who do so can often end up hurting themselves or act out. For example, they may hit a sibling when they try to take something from their hand. Since they don't know anything better, they react in whatever means they seem fit. Your child may want to skip school because they are being bullied at school and can't think of a better way to make it stop. So they avoid attending school altogether, hoping this would keep their bully at bay. However, as a parent, you must know that such impulsiveness can lead to bigger problems in the longer run.

Learning to problem-solve helps young ones distinguish what a solvable problem is. They can understand better the cause and effect of things. They can learn to become responsive instead of reacting on impulse. It will make them think critically, become more reflective of their actions, and develop grit. When they are left to tackle problems on their own, they feel empowered to think and come up with a course of action. They can view challenges from a fresh perspective and take calculated risks.

When they can do that; the likelihood of success increases significantly.

The 5 Stages of Problem-Solving

Kids can feel overwhelmed when they are unable to address a problem. However, if they know what steps they must follow to tackle it properly, they can feel more competent and in control. They can feel confident in themselves and their abilities and take the risk of trying. Different psychologists, book authors, and relationship experts categorize problem-solving differently. But to keep things simple, here are the five steps to problem-solving that you must teach your child.

1. Problem Identification: The first step involves stating the problem aloud. This helps kids know that they are stuck and come to terms with it.

Stating the problem aloud means you identify that something is bothering you and you must address it.

2. Brainstorm Solutions: The next step includes coming up with at least three solutions that can help kids resolve the issue. They don't have to be sensible or good ideas. Even the most far-fetched and silliest of answers will do as long as it gets the kid thinking and analyzing.

3. Pick One: Once you have laid out different ideas, evaluate which has the most potential to succeed. Encourage the child to pick it.

4. Put it to test: once you have figured out which solution you will move forward with, test it out, and see what happens. If it backfires, go to step 3 and reevaluate your choices.

5. Review: Finally, don't forget to assess the impact of the solution. Review which solution worked and the impact it had.

Every time your child comes up with a problem or issue, let them go through these five steps to resolve it. The more they practice, the more efficient they will become.

Practical Tips to Develop Problem-Solving Skills

We all face problems of varying kinds. The only difference between us adults and kids is that we can think and analyze them for what they are. Kids can become confused when they get stuck as they are incapable to think and analyze situations like adults. Their mind is still in the developmental stages and thus, things like challenges, stress, and complication don't make sense to them. Some days, it can be a toy-related conflict, and other days, negative peer pressure.

As parents, we can't be with our kids all the time, which is why they must learn to survive on their own and rely on their instincts to guide them better. Teaching them to overcome obstacles and resolve complicated issues they face daily can make them confident, successful, and self-reliant individuals—the very qualities of a great leader. So how can you help them develop and hone their problem-solving skills? Here are a few ideas.

When you face a challenge yourself, think-aloud of what you must do, especially when your child is in the same room. Go through the five steps discussed earlier, ensuring that your child notices you. Children are impressionable. They learn from us and our actions. When they see us solving issues logically and rationally, they will adopt a similar strategy too. There is no better teacher than real-world examples kids can use for their good.

You can also pretend to not have a solution and invite your kids to come up with some. Ask them for advice on how you should proceed and see what ideas they put forth. This is yet another activity to engage and teach children how to address their problems.

Whichever ideas they come up with, no matter how insensible, appreciate them. Appreciate them for being an active participant and value the ideas they shared. When they feel important, included, and valued this way, they will be more receptive to modeling the same behaviors when they face problems.

Moreover, when teaching about problem-solving, don't always provide them with the answer right away. Motivate them to brainstorm and decide which solution is the best one. Again, the goal is to appreciate them for the effort and encourage repetition.

If they go with a solution that isn't right or suitable, don't stop them. Let them try and let them fail. Make them face the consequences too so that they know they will always be held accountable for their actions and behaviors. This is a little harsh but also necessary.

Instill the "what if…" mindset. Let them test new approaches by questioning traditional methods. Help them see things from a different perspective so that they may expand their knowledge.

Chapter 6:

Leaders Adhere to

Principles

Adherence to principles means staying committed and devoted to making a difference. Not everyone can do so but there are many great examples we can learn from.

When Albert Einstein was in school, he was one of the dullest children in his class. His teachers thought he was retarded. Little did they know that the retarded boy would soon go on to become one of the biggest names in the world. By the time Einstein turned 26, he already obtained his Ph.D. He also submitted four important papers on mass-energy equivalence topics. However, his papers and research were rejected and ignored until his contribution $E=MC2$ shocked the scientific community. He had a vivid imagination, perseverance, and an unbending will. He questioned everything, even his beliefs but stayed committed to moving forward. Even in his final days in the office, he was pictured as a man with great conviction and dedication towards his work.

The example of Richard Branson is no different. Richard Branson may be known as the owner of the Virgin group of companies, but not many are aware of the many failed expansion projects that should have made him call it quits. But despite those failures, he remained committed to staying afloat and adapting to changing circumstances with his razor-sharp focus and attention to the latest trends.

In an overstimulated and distracted society, we need to give our children ample opportunities to develop self-control and focus. In today's world, our attention spans have reduced to less than three seconds. Kids, who are oozing energy and exploring the world around them, have a hard time sitting down and remaining engaged, let alone stay focused. But if we learn anything from the examples of the great leaders mentioned above, it is this: their attention, focus, and persistent conviction are what earned them a forever place in the hearts of the people.

This next chapter explores another one of the many traits of great leaders and how we can teach our children to become more committed to their dreams and ambitions in life by improving their focus and concentration. But before we do that, let's understand what poor focus looks like and the impact it has on a child's mind.

What Poor Focus Looks Like

When a child is unable to focus or concentrate, say on their homework or in class, only then can you understand the repercussions it comes with. The child suffers mentally when they fail to grasp basic concepts or recall them later. It can also threaten their friendships as they fail to give others the attention they deserve and drive them away. It can make doing simple tasks difficult and impossible which can end in anger and frustration. Poor focus and concentration also lead to procrastination which is setting things off for another day or time. This is one of the many signs that a child is unable to focus and therefore, shows a lack of interest in the activity or the task. Other things you should look at include:

Struggling to follow through on basic things and tasks like homework

Losing interest in things quicker than others and wanting to move onto the next activity or task

Needing to be stimulated constantly aka being reminded of what they are doing and what is expected of them

Daydream and remain lost in their trail of thoughts

Being unable to remember what is being said minutes ago because their mind wasn't focused

Have difficulty adapting to any new changes in their lives like a new school, class, or place

Remaining disorganized and unable to find their things

On the other hand, children who can self-regulate their emotions and remain focused can prevent themselves from becoming distracted and finish all tasks and activities successfully. They also exhibit a higher sense of self-efficacy. They are more excited about going to school, making new friends, or visiting new places. They can resist distractions and prevent putting things off. They also tend to be happier as they are fully aware of what they want from life and have a clear idea of where they are headed and what they must do to get there.

How to Improve Focus

Ever noticed how flexible, toned, and ripped our muscles become with regular exercise? Concentration is a muscle that can be strengthened with exercise. Some kids are naturally able to and sustain focus. Others need some help with it. Thankfully, there are several parenting books, articles, and blogs online that can help parents improve their child's poor concentration and attention skills.

Razor-sharp focus is something that affects different areas of a child's life. It helps them achieve good grades in school, follow their dreams and passions fearlessly, and be who they are. It is one thing to stay focused on activities that are interesting and engaging and another when they are boring and tedious. The ability to focus and sustain an optimal level of attention in such situations is the real test. Being able to sustain focus helps children expand their knowledge, improve, and become more self-assured. So how can you help them achieve a razor-sharp focus so that they can be successful in all endeavors of their life? Take a look below.

Make instructions clear and expectations real. One of the most effective ways to improve focus is by ensuring that what you have communicated has been well-received by the receiver. If you sense any confusion, ask them to repeat the instructions to you so that you two can be at the same pace.

Read them stories so that they can expand their attention span by remaining focused and engaged in it. to further promote the idea, have a question-answer session after the book is finished and discussed all that has been read. This way, you will know which characters, situations, or experiences interest them the most and you can take note of it.

Promote pretend play. Pretend play or role playing allows you two to act and pretend to be different people. Staying focused is the key as both the players have to stay in the roles and act how a particular character would act. Role-playing also improves cognitive flexibility as it allows children to be creative and express themselves.

Encourage goal-setting. Children can only focus and concentrate better when they have the steps laid out for them to follow. This requires the creation of daily action plans and goal setting because goal setting firms up a child's mind to achieve something. It helps them streamline and prioritize their actions better and avoid procrastinating or getting distracted.

Speaking of distractions, avoid offering them many when trying to improve their focus and concentration. Reduce background noises and other external distractions that take away their attention. When doing something important, set-up a serious and distraction-free environment so that the child can concentrate better.

Let them guess and come up with answers and ideas themselves. Meaning; engage them in activities and games that encourage creativity and imagination. Come up with random, self-made games without any rules or expectations. Better yet, create your own rules based on what your child can come up with. You can also change rules halfway and see if your child follows through or not, proving how focused or unfocused they are.

Chapter 7:

Leaders Are Honest and

Honorable

Another great quality that great leaders possess is honesty and honor. All influential people are honest in their ways and actions. They don't deceive people or lead them astray. They are committed to speaking the truth and only the truth, even if that makes them the bad guy.

As parents, modeling honesty is one of the most important skills to teach young children. They are naturally honest but lie when they feel they will have to face harsh consequences such as punishment, getting their privileges taken away, or grounded.

All parents want to raise honest and honorable kids. We have faith in them and believe that they will do no wrong. But can we be certain of their actions and behaviors when they aren't in front of us? There are several reasons that kids lie, the most important being getting away with punishment. Other reasons include gaining approval from loved ones, testing out new behaviors, bragging and showing off, or seeking attention.

Whichever is the reason, honesty and transparency can't be stressed enough as it lays the foundation of every personal and professional relationship they build. To enable them to cherish their loved ones and be valued in return, be listened to and be understood, and most importantly, to become leaders others can rely upon, we must make efforts to channel honesty and honor in them.

Luckily, this chapter looks closely at honesty and transparency and how can parents model them.

The Importance of Transparency and Honesty

I recall the time when my child came up to me and lied straight to my face that he would like to drop out of their school's football team because the teacher was mean to him. After noticing how terrible he felt after every practice session and avoided having to chat about how his day went, I reached out to the teacher only to discover that his reasons for wanting to quit were entirely different. He wanted to quit because he wanted to join the drama club instead but was afraid to come clean because he feared the reaction he would get from me or everyone else in his class. He was the broody kind and everyone assumed that he would make an excellent addition to the football team.

After coming home, I stayed in my room for hours because I felt betrayed. I thought we were the best of buds. We both loved to watch sports together and I assumed that he had an interest in it. So I pushed him to try out and he got in. But now, he was lying to me because he didn't want to let me down or live in the fear that I would be against his decision to quit.

So when he came home, we had an in-depth discussion about how important it is, to be honest, and be fearless to choose what they want.

Had I not talked to the teacher and known the reasons behind the desire to quit, I would have never known. The reason I share this with you is that our kid lies. Their intentions may be different but most of the time it is because they are fearful of our reactions and responses.

But that shouldn't stop us from modeling honesty. If anything, it should encourage us further to become better parents and raise them, to be honest with themselves and others.

Raising Honorable Humans – It All Begins With Being Honest

So how can you teach them to be honest and transparent with you and others? Here are a few ideas.

Praise them when they tell the truth: Rewarding the truth is an integral step to encouraging honesty. We are quick to scold and say no to our kids. We rush to prove them wrong, belittle, and mock them for being stupid. So they start to hide things from us. Sadly, we rarely praise them when they do something good or come clean about a mistake they made or a lie they said. Aim to discipline them positively by being kind and approachable. Reward behaviors that you want to see more of and ignore the ones that are bad and unwanted.

Be a role model by telling the truth always. This can't be stressed enough. Don't shower them or others with false praises when you know you have a little one noticing and scrutinizing all your actions. Don't let them catch you telling a lie. Model honesty in your actions and words and your little one will do the same.

Offer forgiveness when they come clean about a lie they told in the past. The very reason they approached you is that they want you to understand and show empathy. Therefore, unless it is something grave, forgive and console them. Remind them that they can always come to you with any problems they face instead of lying about them and acting as if everything is fine.

Don't test them to lie to you. Sometimes, we parents test our children by asking them questions they wouldn't want to answer. For example, if they are a teenager or recently started dating someone, repeatedly questioning them about their love interest when they don't want to discuss it yet, is giving them a chance to lie to you. Therefore, avoid paying too much in their life or trying to control it. it too gives them a chance to lie and get away with it.

Have them face the consequences of being dishonest. They should know that their parents won't always save them from punishment. If they don't do their homework and lie to their teacher, let them know how it will affect their overall grade. If they lie to you about brushing their teeth, let them suffer through the pain of a toothache. Appropriate disciplining is another way to model honesty in them so that they know that even if they lie, they can't run away from it.

Follow through on your promises. A child will only trust you if you do as you say or committed to doing. Children should regard your word and actions as sacred and look up to you as an authority figure. Not following through with your promises depicts you not only as a liar but also as untrustworthy. Therefore, when trying to raise honest and transparent toddlers, teenagers, and one day, adults, let them know that you can always be trusted.

Once they are honest and transparent, they will become honorable because they won't have to concoct or make things up. When they will have nothing to hide, they can come clean and present their arguments with confidence. They will also become better listeners as they will be drawn towards honesty in others too. They will remain committed to their word and follow through with their promises. All great leaders are honest in their quests. They don't try to cheat their followers or break their trust by spreading a net of lies. They understand the value of trust and therefore, are determined to keep everything clear. They know that if they fall short on their promises and fail to deliver, they will lose their expertise and reputation.

Chapter 8:

Leaders are Empathetic

and Humble

It might seem a little odd to include a religious leader in the book but Dalai Lama has surely earned his place as one of the most inspirational and empowering personalities there is. He has led many peaceful protest movements during his political career. He was awarded the Nobel Peace Prize in 1989 for his resistance against the Chinese rule in Tibet in a non-violent manner. Today, he has been forced to live in exile due to his strong stance on issues like the environment, economics, religion, science, and even women's rights. What he is known for is his peace, tolerance, and compassion towards all.

Another truly inspirational personality without whom, the book would remain incomplete is Mandela. Standing side by side with Luther King Jr., Nelson Mandela fought in the pursuit of getting south Africa rid of its apartheid regime. Being imprisoned for life, he spent twenty-seven years in prison for enticing young workers to unite and strike against the government to end apartheid. During his time in jail, he earned a degree, demonstrated hunger and work strikes, met with several political leaders, and wrote his autobiography about how he would sacrifice his life if apartheid continued in the south afraid. He was tortured in his cell repeatedly but didn't give up on his goal. His spirits were never broken and after getting released from prison in 1990, he was elected the first-ever black leader of the country.

What their life portrays is the life of a humble, honest, and empathetic person. They put their people first, suffered because of them, sacrificed the most splendid time of their life, their youth, to bring justice and peace to others. Their whole life is a testament to what it is like to live for others, something that holds great importance, especially today.

Today's society isn't a promising one. We are leaving our children on a planet with poor natural resources, air and water pollution, genetically-modified foods, several diseases that were never even discussed in broad daylight at homes, and whatnot. With racial inequality on the rise and people killing one another for sport, having empathy and humility is an essential and valuable skill to have. All great leaders embodied empathy and humility.

This chapter looks at the final two qualities of great leaders, tied together. The power of humility and empathy in life and why all great future leaders must have it if they wish to change the world for the better. First, let's explore the two concepts in-depth and see if they stand for the same thing or not.

What Is Empathy And Humbleness?

Humility is often used synonymously in place of modesty but it isn't always about it. Humility isn't pretending to be someone you are not or more specifically, pretending to be less. People who practice humility are one of the few who have high self-worth. They recognize their strengths, weaknesses, and limitations. There is research that poses a strong connection between humility and generosity. Children in modern society are rewarded for being narcissistic. The media tells them that it is okay to take a hundred selfies per day, show off their valued assets, and take pride when posting it online using a dozen filters. It seems that being humble, respectful, and appreciative of who we are is outdated.

But if we look at its impact in the longer run, we don't need any research to confirm what lays ahead a mentally-unstable individual that relies on others for validation. This makes humility a quality to value and develop in children. Humility is putting others first. A humble person thinks less of himself and more of others. They are confident, approachable, and respectful of others' personal space and belief systems. They aren't arrogant, or forceful. They don't seek validation from others for what they do or don't do. They rely on themselves and themselves alone.

Empathy, on the other hand, is the ability to lend someone different from you, your understanding. It means putting yourself in their shoes and viewing the world from their eyes. It involves active listening and being present for others. It is about hearing them out and understanding what they are going through. It includes taking note of not just what is being said but how it is being said. To see empathy in action, have you ever been late to the office and have your boss come up to you and tell you that it happens to everyone and that you shouldn't worry about it? Or perhaps, you are sad and pour out your heart to someone and they tell you that they understand what you are going through?

Well, that's empathy. It is different from humility but an important aspect of it.

How to Connect Better and Build Meaningful Relationships

Since the goal is to preach empathy and humility, what better way to begin with looking at both working in unison?

To practice both humility and empathy, we must start with stepping outside our comfort zones and then also outside our tribes. To be empathetic and humble, we must forget who we are or where we come from. We all want to be surrounded by like-minded people. The only drawback is that it limits our perspective about the world. We only see what we want to see as we are surrounded by a certain definition of what life is like. Therefore, the first step is the hardest and entails that we step out and leave behind all the comforts we know of and also the people that have a special space in our lives. We need to engage with those with a different view of life, who act and think differently. This is necessary because it allows us to see things in a different light and know that our knowledge is limited about the world. Acknowledging that you don't have all the answers is humility and acknowledging that you can make a difference and fill those gaps is empathy. Humility reminds us that we can't do everything on our own or for ourselves and empathy introduces us to the challenges that others have faced. When we combine these two, we can invite ourselves into meaningful and authentic relationships with everyone and collaborate with them to trigger change.

Empathy encourages us to unite and humility keeps us open to new knowledge, wisdom, and insights.

Kids of today, especially teenagers, are overconfident. They think they know everything about the world and all that goes in it. They have strong opinions about how they view the world and believe it to be the only truth there is. They have a hard time accepting when confronted with a different viewpoint. The only measuring stick they recognize is themselves. They think only they are in the right and the rest of the world is in the wrong. This kind of thinking breeds arrogance, the opposite of humility. But the world already has enough arrogance. How about we seek humility and empathy for a change? Here are several ways to impart this wisdom and teach your child to become humble in their ways and empathetic about others.

Model positive behavior. Always aim to teach through example and experiences. Surely, you must have stories about how empathy can change one's viewpoint and help one see under the layers of one's actions and behaviors. Present them with those examples and model the same with them too. Meaning, when they come up to you to share a grievance or simply talk, listen with openness and without judgment to let them know that you can be trusted. Refrain from offering unsolicited advice unless asked for. Tell them that humility isn't a skill but a lifestyle that they must adapt if they want to be loved by all.

Reward their actions when they portray humbleness. Never let a teachable or recognizable moment pass by because believe it or not but humility comes from a place of strength, belief, and self-assurance. So build them up, celebrate their little acts of kindness, and boast about their empathetic qualities in front of others to promote the behavior.

Don't humiliate them, especially in a vulnerable moment when they seek guidance and comfort from you. Just because you want them to be humble doesn't mean you must bully them or beat them down into developing it. If they are repeatedly failing to put others before them, don't humiliate or belittle them.

Expose them to the lives of the greatest leaders who were the embodiment of humility and empathy. Read to them about great and selfless personalities like Mother Teresa, Jesus Christ, Mahatma Gandhi, etc., to put forth real-life examples of people who lived for others.

Volunteer to charitable organizations and community shelters. This will give them a taste of what it is like to serve. Hopefully, the experience will be life-changing for them and they will begin to value the little things in life they had been taking for granted for so long. Also, it will build the habit of looking after one another.

Show them how to apologize. To be humble, children must know how to apologize when they are in the wrong and accept that they made a mistake. Acknowledgment of their mistakes leads to correcting them and avoiding them in the future.

Teach them to be grateful for what they have and not take things for granted. Being grateful is the cornerstone of humility. Without gratitude and appreciation for life, good health, money, and safety, children can never learn the value of it all. Therefore, encourage them to use words like "please" and "thank you" as much as possible so that they can develop a habit of being gracious. You can also ask them to keep a gratitude journal and every day, list one thing they are grateful for in their lives. A humble and simple gesture as such will make them value things more and be accountable for how they use them.

Conclusion

Parenting is hard, especially when you have to spell out every request and ensure that you have been heard carefully. It comes with its challenges but the biggest one is related to their decent upbringing. Our children are an extension of us, which is why; we often expect them to be perfect. We put up certain rules and regulations for them to abide by, say yes to every request we make, and behave well-mannered.

But why expect them to be perfect when they can be imperfect and still great?

Only robots and machines are perfect. Humans aren't and never have been. So instead of trying to channel perfection in them, how about we try to raise them as sensible, obedient, honest, and self-reliant individuals? How about we raise them to be leaders and lead others with their wisdom and expertise, their charisma and charm, their devotion and conviction, their razor-sharp focus, humility, and empathy instead?

Surely, these are some of the best qualities and skills to develop in them. In this book, we looked at seven such qualities and skills which if taught right, can raise a generation of future leaders who are ready to challenge the status quo and demand betterment for all.

In times like these, we can only hope that a better future awaits and our little contribution can be our children who grow up to lead others to success, happiness, and improved well-being.

Thank you for reading my book, I hope you enjoyed it as much as I enjoyed writing it. Please visit the site where you purchased it and take a moment to write an honest and brief review. Your feedback is important to me. Even just a few words would help others decide if the book is right for them. Best regards and thank you in advance.

References

6 ways to help your child focus. (2019, August 5).
Understood.org; Understood.
https://www.understood.org/en/learning-
thinking-differences/child-learning-
disabilities/add-adhd/how-to-improve-focus-
in-kids

10 of the most inspiring leaders of all time: Remarkable
stories of iconic trail blazers who went from
adversity to extraordinary & redefined
leadership. (2019, August 5). Inspiring
Leadership Now.
https://www.inspiringleadershipnow.com/mos
t-inspiring-leaders-redefine-leadership/

10 ways to teach your children humility. (2010, August
5). All pro Dad.
https://www.allprodad.com/10-ways-to-teach-
your-children-humility/

10 ways to teach your children to be honest. (2010, July
30). All pro Dad.
https://www.allprodad.com/10-ways-to-teach-
your-children-to-be-honest/

30 life changing benefits of positivity | 10 minute read.
(2020, April 20). Power of Positivity: Positive

Thinking & Attitude.
https://www.powerofpositivity.com/positivity-life-changing-benefits/

Biasotto, K. (2019, May 20). How to raise a child who can think out of the box and survive in any situation. A Fine Parent. https://afineparent.com/positive-parenting-faq/critical-thinkers.html

Carter, K. (n.d.). 5 reasons why great leaders are made not born. Motivii. https://www.motivii.com/blog/great-leaders-born-made

Childress, J. (2017, April 27). Leadership can't be taught, but it can be learned! Td.org. https://www.td.org/insights/leadership-cant-be-taught-but-it-can-be-learned

Cullins, A. (2020, September). How to teach problem-solving skills to kids (ages 3-14). Big Life Journal. https://biglifejournal.com/blogs/blog/how-teach-problem-solving-strategies-kids-guide#:~:text=Instead%20of%20giving%20up%20or

Gillespie, P. (2017, May 24). Intuit: Gig economy is 34% of US workforce. CNNMoney. http://money.cnn.com/2017/05/24/news/economy/gig-economy-intuit/index.html

Hall, J. (2018, April 29). 5 ways to raise your kids to be better leaders and entrepreneurs. Forbes. https://www.forbes.com/sites/johnhall/2018/04/29/5-ways-to-raise-your-kids-to-be-better-leaders-and-entrepreneurs/?sh=732f54f69b39

Hurley, K. (2016). How to build resilience in children: Strategies to strengthen your kids. Psycom.net - Mental Health Treatment Resource since 1986. https://www.psycom.net/build-resilience-children

James. (2019, April 22). The power of humility and empathy – the arc. The Arc. https://www.tyndale.com/sites/readthearc/the-power-of-humility-and-empathy/

Levens, S. M., & Gotlib, I. H. (2012). The effects of optimism and pessimism on updating emotional information in working memory. Cognition & Emotion, 26(2), 341–350. https://doi.org/10.1080/02699931.2011.574110

Morgan, J. (2020, January 6). What is leadership, and who is a leader? Chief Learning Officer - CLO Media. https://www.chieflearningofficer.com/2020/01/06/what-is-leadership-and-who-is-a-leader/#:~:text=A%20leader%20is%20someone%20who%20can%20see%20how%20things%20can

Morin, A. (2019). Teach kids how to solve their own problems and make good decisions. Verywell Family. https://www.verywellfamily.com/teach-kids-problem-solving-skills-1095015

Okafor, J. (n.d.). What are the benefits of a positive attitude? Keeping a positive attitude. TRVST. https://www.trvst.world/inspiration/what-are-the-benefits-of-a-positive-attitude/

Pelini, S. (2017, May 29). 10 evidence-backed tips to teach kids focus and concentration. Raising-Independent-Kids. https://raising-independent-kids.com/10-evidence-backed-tips-teach-kids-focus-concentration/#:~:text=Several%20studies%20have%20found%20that

Resilience guide for parents and teachers. (2012, January 24). Apa.org. https://www.apa.org/topics/resilience/guide-parents-teachers

Rymanowicz, K. (2016, April 19). The importance of focus and self-control for young children. MSU Extension. https://www.canr.msu.edu/news/the_importance_of_focus_and_self_control_for_young_children#:~:text=Focus%20and%20self%2Dcontrol%20are%20essential%20skills%20for%20life.&text=Studies%20have%20shown%20that%20children

Sarkhedi, B. (2020, August 18). Importance of having a positive attitude in life. Times of India Blog. https://timesofindia.indiatimes.com/readersblo g/thereality/importance-of-having-a-positive-attitude-in-life-24763/

Sims, L. (n.d.). The importance of concentration in a child's development | nelson realty. Nelson Realty. Retrieved February 27, 2021, from http://www.nelsonrealty.net/the-importance-of-concentration-in-a-childs-development/

Syahrial, Dr., Asrial, Dr., Sabil, H., & Arsil, Dr. (2020). Attitudes, self-confidence, and independence of students in thematic learning. Universal Journal of Educational Research, 8(1), 162–168. https://doi.org/10.13189/ujer.2020.080120

Sykes, T. (2019, January 10). Why you need to think outside the box. Entrepreneur. https://www.entrepreneur.com/article/325989 #:~:text=Perhaps%20one%20of%20the%20m ost

Teach children to think outside of the box. (2018, September 20). Growing Play. https://www.growingplay.com/2018/09/teach-children-to-think-outside-of-the-box/

The 10 most inspirational people of all time. (2020, January 23). The Gentleman's Journal. https://www.thegentlemansjournal.com/most-inspirational-people/

Thompson, H. (2019, November 27). Born or led into greatness? How to raise leaders from a young age. BOSS Magazine. https://thebossmagazine.com/raising-leaders/

Tracy, B. (2008, January 21). Leaders are made, not born. Brian Tracy's Self Improvement & Professional Development Blog. https://www.briantracy.com/blog/leadership-success/leaders-are-made-not-born/#:~:text=Fortunately%2C%20leaders%2 0are%20made%2C%20not

Tugade, M. M., Fredrickson, B. L., & Feldman Barrett, L. (2004). Psychological resilience and positive emotional granularity: Examining the benefits of positive emotions on coping and health. Journal of Personality, 72(6), 1161–1190. https://doi.org/10.1111/j.1467-6494.2004.00294.x

Wagner, D. (2017, November 3). 4 tools to help kids develop empathy and cultural humility. KQED. https://www.kqed.org/mindshift/49609/4-tools-to-help-kids-develop-empathy-and-cultural-humility

Why is problem solving important in child development? (2020, March 19). Www.marlborough.org. https://www.marlborough.org/news/~board/health-and-wellness/post/why-is-problem-solving-important-in-child-development

Why you always need to be thinking outside of the box. (2013, March 5). Elite Daily. https://www.elitedaily.com/money/entreprene urship/thinking-box

Williams, P. (2016, November 7). Helping your kids develop humility. Focus on the Family. https://www.focusonthefamily.com/parenting/ helping-your-kids-develop-humility/

Made in the USA
Middletown, DE
16 August 2021

46213672R00044